HOW TO WEAR SOCKS

HOW TO WEAR SOCKS

JOHN JANNUZZI

ILLUSTRATIONS BY
MIKE LEMANSKI

Abrams Image, New York

CONTENTS

Introduction

If you rolled your eyes at the title of this book, I'm not exactly surprised. Socks, a bare necessity of any person's wardrobe, are often an afterthought, a one-and-done, wear-it-if-it's-clean kind of garment. You put them on, pull them up, and go about the rest of your day. And yes, that's all true! But there's a lot more to a good sock than meets the eye, and there's so much they can do for your vibe.

Within the galaxy of socks, there's a staggering amount of options, from material to style to, of course, more obvious things like color and print. There are famous socks, and there are non-famous ones, there are socks for running, socks for sitting, socks for sleeping, socks for weddings, socks for babies, and, at one point or another, even socks for getting buried in. (Sorry to be the bearer of bad news, but death comes for us all. And I bet the grim reaper has socks, too.)

And lest we forget, thanks to the endless imagination of mankind, socks aren't just for feet. There are the odd practical uses for cleaning or storing loose change, and then the more creative applications (looking at you, Red Hot Chili Peppers).

So as you can see, there's quite a lot to socks. There are things to keep in mind as you build up your perfect sock arsenal, style tips you never knew you needed (socks with sandals—try it!), very specific ways to care for your favorite pairs, and tips on how to repair them. There's a whole sock world out there—a universe, even! And it's worth exploring.

And if you're still rolling your eyes, this book will make an excellent paperweight, and I won't be offended if it sits on your toilet tank for years to come.

CHAPTER ONE

The Basics

A BRIEF HISTORY OF SOCKS

We're not born with socks, so where did they come from? Well, they've been around for centuries, with the earliest versions simply being animal hides that were gathered up around the feet. (Cozy.) Of course, things evolved, but not much has changed over time. After all, a good sock is a good sock, animal hides or not.

Ancient Greek Sock Ancestors

An early relative of socks called *piloi* were mentioned in the poet Hesiod's didactic poem *Work and Days*. These aren't the kinds of things you'd want to see in a department store, though. They were made of matted animal hair—not something you'd ever want to throw on with a pair of sneakers. But it's important to remember where you came from, right? And these bad boys came from the eighth century BC—OGs, you might say.

The Mummy of Socks

The oldest pair of socks in existence dates all the way back to 300–500 AD, and aside from some wear and tear, the structure is very similar to what we've got today. You might even think of them as a statement sock with their bright color and funky split toe. By the way, that toe is split so the ancient Egyptians could wear them with their sandals. (A debate as old as time, apparently.) They're currently residing at the Victoria and Albert Museum in London—do not attempt to wear them, please.

TIP

"There are people with a certain type of cool who can pull off socks with sandals. . . . You are not one of them (myself included)."
—Jamie Beck, photographer

Socks Go Roman

If you hopped to Rome around the same time, you'd also find some sock-like garments. These were called *udones*, a type of wrapping that the Romans would put around their feet, usually made of leather or woven fabrics. These eventually became a more familiar version of what we know today and were popular among soldiers for protection from the cold.

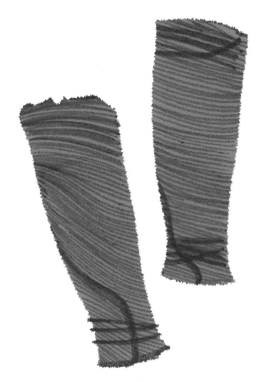

Holy Feet

In the fifth century, holy people in Europe wore *puttees*, which were meant to symbolize purity. These were long pieces of cloth that were wrapped around the lower part of the leg, and they later became popular with various militaries across the world to ensure good foot health. After all, you can't march with unclean feet and legs. (Quite a pivot.)

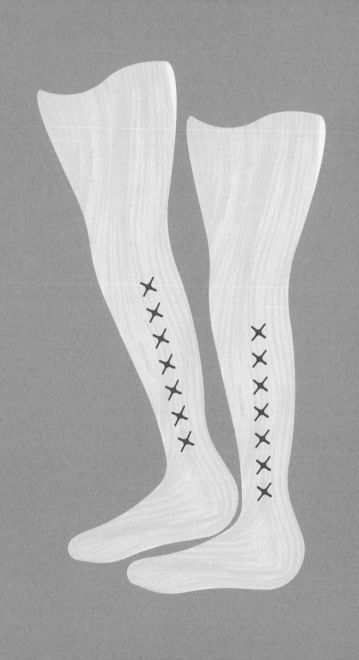

Status Socks

Fast-forward a bit (think 1000 AD), and wearing socks becomes more of a status symbol for the highfalutin people of the world. Because this was technically "the olden days," the making of socks and stockings was far more painstaking than it is today. That labor, along with bright colors, fine materials like silk, and ornamentation added to the cost of manufacturing, keeping things exclusive. If you look at old (like Middle Ages old) artwork, you can observe a lot of figures with crowns and nice leggings, usually held up by garters. Wealth!

Mass Production, Sort Of

Socks remained largely unchanged until two significant moments occurred that shifted everything. The first came in 1589 with the invention of the knitting machine, which would allow socks to be made much faster and more efficiently, though this method of production was slightly ahead of its time and didn't truly take off until the early nineteenth century.

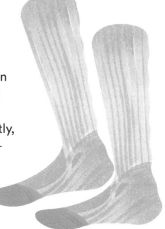

The Big Nylon Breakthrough

Though methods of production had advanced, it wasn't until 1938 that the true big breakthrough happened—that breakthrough being nylon. The stretch, comfort, and ease of the material were wildly popular when it first debuted at the 1939 World's Fair, and today's materials are mostly the same. So long, garters; hello, friendly elastics.

The Socks of Today

With manufacturing handled on all ends, the world of socks really opened up. The stocking-like garments of antiquity were produced in the thousands, tube socks hit the scene, short ones, long ones, printed ones, and all kinds flourished between then and now. We've come a long way from wrapping our feet with dead animals. And thank god—nobody wants to be wearing matted squirrel socks at the gym.

Sock Anatomy

THE WELT: The top part of your sock that's generally a little thicker than the rest. It's usually ribbed to help keep things from falling down and into your shoe (the worst).

THE RIB: Everything between the very top of your sock and the top of your ankle. It's essentially the tube of a tube sock.

THE BOOT: Socks have their own boots. Who knew? This area is the no-man's-land between the heel and the rib. It's what covers that part of your foot that always gets torn up when breaking in new shoes (also the worst).

THE HEEL: A crucial part of any sock. And yes, as you've probably guessed, it covers your heel. It also creates a better fit when appropriately sized.

THE FOOT OR FOOTBED: Much of a sock's value is to be found in the footbed, where extra cushioning can provide more comfort and ease. It's the area between your toes and your heel and is generally souped-up in athletic socks.

THE TOE: You guessed it. Please put your five little piggies right in there. Occasionally there is a seam here (which, warning, can cause discomfort), but more modern production methods have been able to eliminate that.

THE CLOCK: Ding-dong! This is just another phrase for the design on the outside of a sock. The term's been used since the sixteenth century. How peculiar.

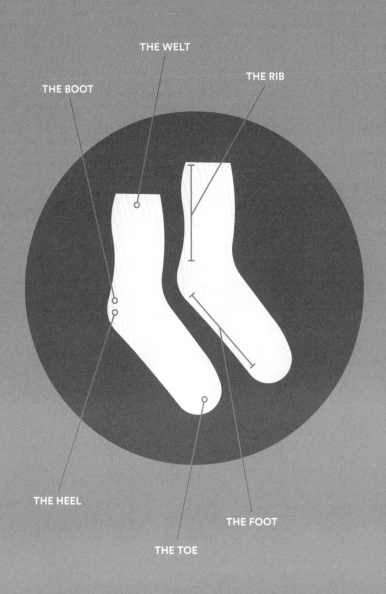

THE WELT

THE BOOT

THE RIB

THE HEEL

THE TOE

THE FOOT

HOW TO PUT ON SOCKS

There's nothing quite like the exhilaration of putting on a pair of socks. They're clean (hopefully)! They're comfy! They're plush! You can slide around wooden floors in them! But if this is the first time you've ever worn them and you're concerned as to how to put them on, follow these simple steps.

Step 1: Grasp one sock firmly in your hand. Look at it with intention. You are going to put it on, and you're going to look great. If you're planning on wearing some tight pants, make sure you do this before putting them on to avoid a dreaded sock line.

Step 2: Prepare your foot. If you're seated, which I recommend, gently lift your leg so your foot is floating gracefully in the air.

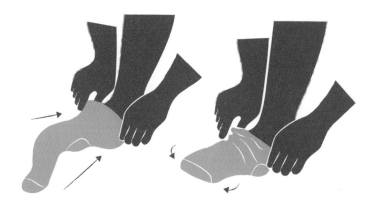

Step 3: Gently pull the welt of the sock around your toes and the bottom of your foot. If you need a break, you can pause here, as the sock should be secure. Maybe have a glass of water.

Step 4: We're back in action. Using the appropriate amount of force, gather the sock around the arch of your feet until your toes are at the end of the sock. Make sure everything is aligned here—you don't want them to get twisted in your shoes.

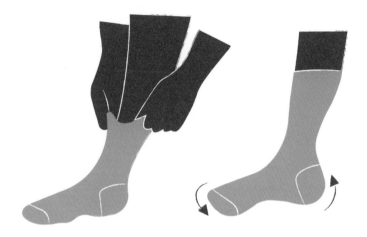

Step 5: Pinch the left and right sides of the top of the sock and pull them up your leg until they are tight around your calf. This step may be unnecessary, depending on the length of your sock.

Step 6: Now that you're almost there, be sure to check that your heel and toes are in the correct spots. Points like this will help keep your socks in place during the day and help you stay nice and comfy.

Step 7: If the rib has become twisted, be sure that any textures line up as vertically as possible. This is crucial to remember for patterned socks but will help with any and every kind of longer version.

Step 8: Repeat steps one through seven for the opposite foot. Eventually, you'll be able to do this without consulting this guide, and pretty soon you'll be able to do the whole thing in about three seconds. Good luck!

CHAPTER TWO

The Key Players

THE TYPES

Now that we're on this sock journey together, it's time to see who else is tagging along. The whos we're speaking about are, of course, all the socks we know. Well, at least the different types. Which kind you wear is truly up to you. Some people like to stick with a classic, while others prefer variety—it is the spice of life, but also the spice of your feet. (I wouldn't recommend putting it in food, though.)

The Tube Sock

A true original. You know it from growing up, from old movies, from *Seinfeld*, and from any store you've ever been to. It's comfortable, it's extra clean, and it often comes with those three stripes right at the top. It's all-purpose and fits in fine in a casual office, a gym, or just a walk around the block. They're available in all manner of lengths, from crew, which will hit you just at the mid-calf, all the way to thigh high, if you're looking for near-total coverage. More often than not, though, they'll hit at the mid-calf. Excellent for sock puppets.

Wear these for binge-watching television, sliding around just-polished floors, casual daily wear.

Brands to Know: Bombas, Nike (particularly Dri-FIT), Hanes

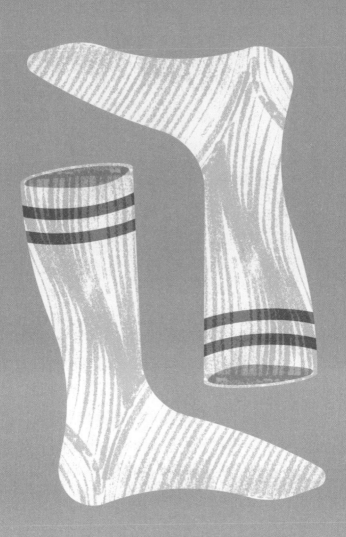

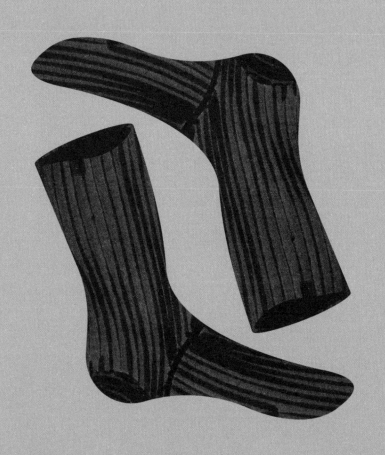

The Standard Sock

These are the ones you can buy at pretty much any clothing store. They're slightly lighter weight than a tube sock but are meant for everyday wear. You can get them in basic solids and neutrals, but there are always stripes, patterns, and designs to be had here. Perfect for the nine-to-five grind. These are most often found in crew lengths—not too short, not too long. They're the building block of a good sock arsenal.

Wear these for any occasion that's neither too fancy, nor too casual; office meetings, meeting the parents.

Brands to Know: Uniqlo, Nice Laundry, Bonobos

The Athletic Sock

An extremely close relative of the classic tube sock, but beefy. It is meant for athletics, after all. Thanks to many modern advancements, these socks are specially outfitted for physical activity. You might find things like moisture-wicking fabric, a little more arch support, or some extra cushioning for all that impact. Even if you're not planning to work out, they're awfully comfortable.

Wear these for any kind of exercise, when you need an extra cushion around the house, setting Olympic records.

Brands to Know: Bombas, Adidas, Nike

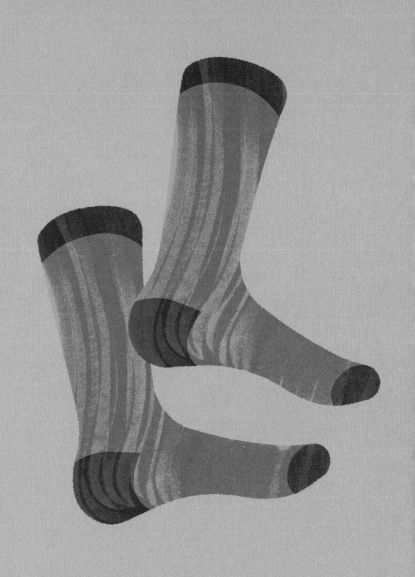

The Boot Sock

Ah, sweet winter. It's the season that promises ever-dryer skin, slushy sidewalks, and, if you're prepared, a good, sturdy pair of boots. Now, there's no law saying that you *must* wear boot socks with boots—if it's not too chilly, that's fine—but when it gets rough out there, these are the move. They're heavier and made from a stronger knit, and will add a nice layer of insulation between you, your boots, and the icy grip of the outdoors.

Wear these for blustery winter days, lumberjack festivals, if you're visiting New England.

Style Tip: This is a matter of personal preference, but you can get away with tucking your pants into your socks here. It saves the hem from the slush and can actually look quite nice, but only if your bottoms are fitted close to your leg. Don't shove a big old hunk of jeans down there.

Brands to Know: L.L.Bean, Uniqlo, Carhartt

The Thermal Sock

It's crucial to know the difference between a thermal and a boot sock. You'll wear both with boots, but thermal socks are meant for true extremes. If you're going on a polar excursion, skiing, snowboarding, or hiking K2, you'll want them. They're very tightly knit and made of highly insulated fibers to keep everything toasty. Just make sure you don't wear them on a regular day; otherwise you'll be sweating through your shoes.

Wear these on the slopes and in the coldest of places.

Brands to Know: Smartwool, Burton, Darn Tough

"The best place to buy winter socks, in my opinion, is sporting good and hiking stores because you'll get the good, thick ones that keep your feet warm all day."
—Tyler McCall, editor in chief of Fashionista.com

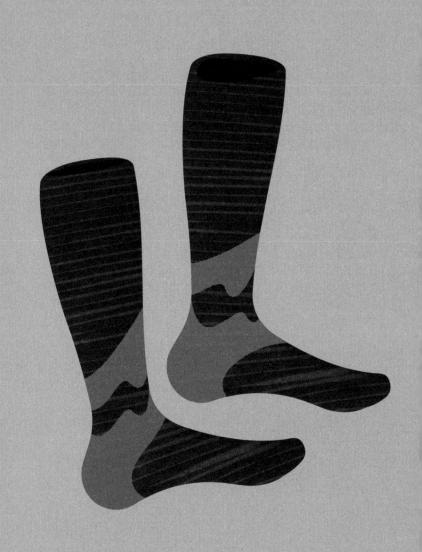

The Compression Sock

These are socks with a little science in them, and they come in many different varieties, all of which have varying degrees of pressure on your ankle and above it. Their main utility is to increase blood flow back up to your heart. You'll often find people wearing these in the gym or some of-the-moment fitness class, but the jury is divided on whether they affect a workout.

Wear these for air travel or when a doctor tells you they might help—particularly after surgery.

Brands to Know: Under Armour, Adidas, Nike

The Knee Sock

Favored by teen queens from Marcia Brady to Cher Horowitz, these are often associated with nostalgia (or school
uniforms). They come in various iterations from casual (like
a regular tube sock) to something a little more dressed up
or fashion-forward made out of finer materials, such as silk,
cashmere, or very fine wool. The one rule, though, is that
they all come up to just below the kneecap.

*Wear these for costume parties, when you're wearing a short
skirt and need some extra warmth/coverage, cosplaying.*

Brands to Know: Wolford, Bombas, ASOS

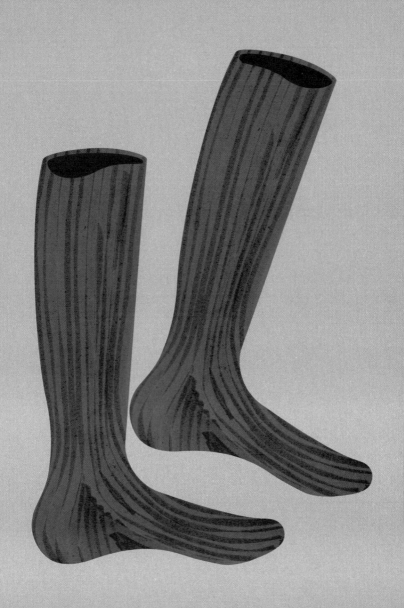

The Ankle Sock

If the athletic sock is a close relative of the tube sock, then this is the, well, shorter one. Ankle socks will either peak out right at the top of your shoes or have a shorter tube that creeps up your leg just a bit. They keep things a little breezier, and if you get the right material, they can go perfectly with a pair of heels.

Wear these for warm, but not too warm days or if you're trying to hide a bad tattoo on your ankle.

Brands to Know: Comme Si, Falke, Uniqlo

The No-Show

If you look at the spectrum of sock history, these are quite new. But they come in very handy. They're designed to keep your feet and your footwear fresh while maintaining the sockless look so many people prefer in the warmer months (we'll get to that in a minute).

Wear these for keeping secrets, tricking people, and when you're afraid of tearing up your feet by going sockless.

Brands to Know: Nice Laundry, Bombas, Vans

"If I *must* wear socks, I like a no-show slipper sock. I'm not nuts for *bold* socks, unless they're tie-dye."
—Laurel Pantin, fashion editor

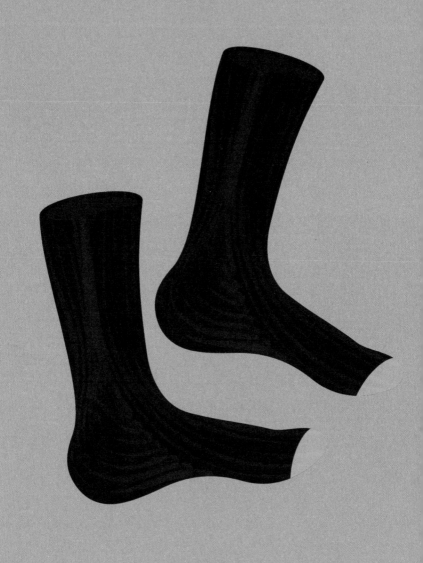

Dress Socks

We've covered most of the casual world, but life is not without its fancy occasions and confusing dress codes, so let's class things up a bit. Socks for special events, commonly known as dress socks, feel more luxurious. Reach for them when you're dressing to the nines, or even the eights. They're lighter, more elegant, and often made from finer materials, such as wool, silk, and cashmere.

Wear these for state dinners, black-tie functions, funerals, weddings.

Brands to Know: Ralph Lauren, Ace & Everett, Bonobos

Statement Socks

Truth be told, any sock can be a statement sock. These are socks that flash a streak of color, a wild print, a bold pattern, or a slogan or imposing logo when you cross your legs or show a little ankle. They're typically favored by quirky aunts, uncles, and pediatricians.

Wear these for attention-seeking, to show that you're "the fun one," or if you're the president of a toy company.

Brands to Know: Happy Socks, Nice Laundry, Stance

TIP

"People always say that the socks are the place to show personality, but I truly think that statement socks are the telltale sign of a fashion victim. A simple stripe or polka dot or speckled sock is all you need."
—Jason Chen, deputy editor, *The Wirecutter*

Fashion-First Socks

Now, these are a very close relative of statement socks, but there's a difference between a sock with clowns printed all over it and something from a fancy designer brand. Everybody from Gucci to Supreme to Vetements has a lineup to offer these days. They can be loud, logo-filled, and just as bold as a regular statement sock, or they can be more standard.

Wear these when you're in any part of Manhattan where there are no numbered streets, at your ritzy high school, or when you're clamoring for attention outside a fashion show.

Brands to Know: Everybody at the top of the list when you sort by high to low price.

The Sockless Play

If you ask me, who happens to be writing this book about socks, my favorite kind of socks is no kind at all. You save a small bit of time and a surprising amount of laundry, and it looks great at a summer wedding. The only snag here is that your shoes will get quite rank after a while, and the oil and sweat from your feet will take its toll on your insoles. Make sure there's baby powder in there, which will help slow that process down a bit. Also, make sure it isn't too cold.

Wear these forever, because they're your feet.

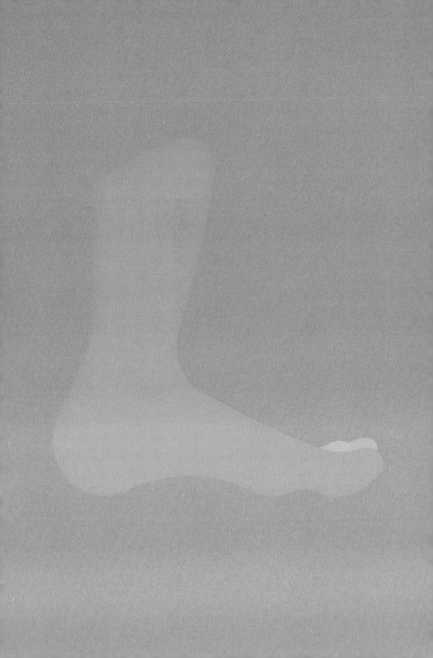

THE LENGTHS

There are so many kinds of socks out there, and lengths aren't exclusive. A tube sock might come in anything from an ankle-length to a thigh-high. You might prefer a trouser-length sock for your dressier occasions, or maybe even a knee-high. But before you make your decision, know the options.

Thigh-High: The tallest of the socks! They tower over any others, and anything longer would just be pants or panty-hose. As the name suggests, these will hit right at the middle of your thigh. Almost complete coverage.

Over-the-Knee: Clock your length down a few inches and you'll be at the over-the-knee zone. These will top off just over your kneecaps for a little extra insulation up top.

Knee-High: The crucial thing to remember about knee-high socks is that they should come up to just below your knee-cap. If you've ever had to wear a school uniform, you know all about these already.

TIP

Leandra Medine Cohen, founder of Man Repeller, goes sockless "only when I'm wearing cropped trousers and loafers and trying to look like an Italian man; otherwise I am a big fan of the calf-length sock, coupled with loafers or sneakers and minidresses and -skirts."

Trouser: We're a few inches south of the knees now, and this is where you start to see more familiar lengths. Trouser socks are slightly longer than a crew length (which is fairly standard) and are a great option for dress socks or more formal use. Though you can feel free to go shorter. Sometimes referred to as tall socks or mid-calf socks.

Crew: The most common length, and the one you probably own the most of. These can land anywhere from the mid-calf to just a few inches below. They're so ubiquitous for a reason—they pair well with nearly every kind of shoe and are perfect for everyday use.

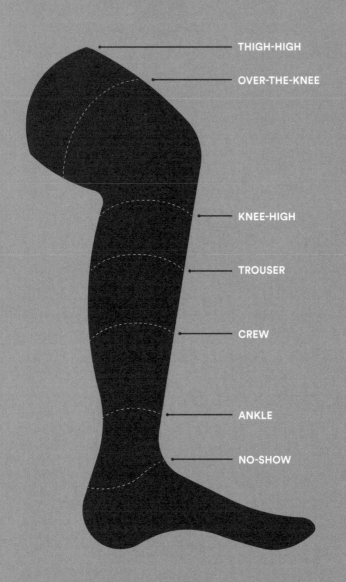

THIGH-HIGH

OVER-THE-KNEE

KNEE-HIGH

TROUSER

CREW

ANKLE

NO-SHOW

Ankle: We'll refer to these as the short stack of the bunch. They'll creep up just an inch or two past the top of your shoes. It's a length that's perfect for athletics or to pair with shorts or a pair of heels (provided you're wearing finer options).

No-Show: These are meant to be invisible and solely exist to provide a barrier between the skin of your feet and your footwear. No-shows are a nice bit of protection to have when you want to go for the sockless look.

"No-show socks are my go-to, but good ones are very hard to find. They must be minimal while also be no-slip, because what is worse than a short sock slipping down and bunching up around your arch? Look for ones with high-quality elastic around the top; they often come in packs of three."
—Elizabeth Holmes, style reporter

MATERIAL

A sock is only as good as its parts. And of course, its parts are made of its materials. More often than not, your socks will have a blend of fibers, such as nylon, polyester, or spandex. These add some durability and elasticity to the whole thing. Chances are you own a healthy mix of everything listed here, but it's always good to know the finer details.

Cotton: Being the fabric of our lives and all, cotton is probably the most commonly used material for socks. It's breathable, comfortable, and readily available. You'll often find it in more garden-variety socks for everyday wear, but it's certainly not exclusive to one type or another.

Bamboo: Derived from the plant itself, bamboo socks offer a little boost of style and comfort. Bamboo is soft and breathable and has a slight sheen, making it a great option for a dress sock or even an everyday one.

Silk: Silk socks aren't the kind of thing you'd want to throw on for a hike or a bike ride. Naturally these are a finer knit, and though they appear fancier, you can mix them up with sneakers or more casual shoes. Because of their light weight, they're ideal for pairing with heels as well.

Wool: Wool is a real game changer, a chameleon of sorts. A heavy wool is great at keeping your feet warm and dry in the winter, and a finer option, like merino, will keep you cool and breezy over the summer. (Merino is also way softer.) Most often your dress socks are made from wool.

TIP

Confused about what to wear when? Follow famous internet person and D-list reality TV star Brian Trunzo's lead: "It's simple for me: cashmere in the winter, artisanal linen/silk/cotton/hemp blends in the summer. It's all about color, mélanges, and texture—not that silly 'show your personality with your socks!'"

Cashmere: Got literal cold feet? Cashmere might be the material to look out for. A thick gauge will have your shivers toasted in no time. Not to mention, of course, cashmere is one of the softest, most luxurious fabrics on the planet. But be warned, it's going to set you back more than your everyday sock. Remember, too, that you can find these in varying weights depending on your needs. (If you're feeling ritzy, try shopping the Elder Statesman, the finest cashmere in the land.)

Acrylic: A commonly used synthetic material for basic socks that's got an intermediate weight and warmth. One major benefit of acrylic is that it retains less moisture than something like cotton, thus providing better wicking.

SO HOW MANY SOCKS DO I NEED?

That's an excellent question, and as much as I'd love to say you need this many of that sock, this many of the other, and that many of none of them, it wouldn't work for everybody. You have to consider your lifestyle and what you personally need. I'd also say that it's really noble to think that you'd do laundry all the time and that you could get away with five or six pairs, but let's be realistic, guys. Think of it in tiers— your go-to/everyday socks, your once-in-a-whiles, and your special occasions. Then you can go out and make some big purchases.

TIP

"Start with classic ribbed crew-length socks in three to five solid colors. Your first sock collection should include neutral colors that you can easily pair with any shoe—black, white, tan—plus a few bolder, brighter colors that allow you to experiment with wearing colorful socks as an accessory. Colored socks can complement your outfit or be the highlight of your outfit; have fun with it."
—Jenni Lee, founder of Comme Si

Go Big for Heavy Rotation: Think of the kind of socks you wear most often. This is going to be where you invest in terms of money, space, and quality. If you need a specific kind of sock on a daily basis, try to net twelve pairs for your rotation. (You'll probably be able to find bundled deals for three pairs at a time, if not more.) If you're hitting the gym every morning and wearing dress socks for the office on the regular, apply the same philosophy to both.

Go Medium for the Supporting Cast: With your most frequent socks taken care of, you can focus on building out the rest. It might sound silly, but life is gonna come at you with some random invites and occasions, and it's always better to be prepared on the sock front. Stock at least three good options of dress socks, basic neutral-colored (they match with everything) everyday socks, and classic white socks at all times. You might wear them seldom, but you'll be glad they're there. You don't have to break the bank here, but make sure you get something that will hold up.

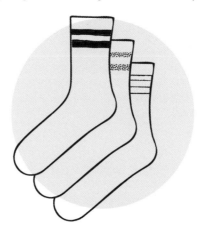

"Navy socks go with 99.9 percent of my dress shoes and loafers, and the bamboo breathes really well."
—Jeremy Kirkland, podcast host and consultant

Go Small for the Rest: With your go-tos and backups sorted, you can start filling out with the more singular options, the pairs that you need only one or two of. Things that might fall into this category: extremely fancy dress socks, souvenir socks from your trip to the Grand Canyon, Christmas socks, etc. Bottom line, you don't want to be relying on a laundry schedule for socks. They take up such little real estate in your drawer (if stored properly) that you can build up a really solid arsenal and always be taken care of.

TIP

"'Fun socks' are not a personality trait."
—James Harris, host of the *Failing Upwards* podcast

CHAPTER THREE

Upkeep and Maintenance

By now, you're well-versed in socks. (You probably were before you got to this chapter, but we're sure of it at this point.) Perhaps you've got a drawer bursting with all different kinds already. Collecting and wearing them is only half the battle here, though. You want to make sure they last as long as possible. And yes, generally, that's just going to mean throwing them in with your regular laundry, but there are a couple of things you can do that will help them last the extra mile.

BRIGHTEN YOUR WHITES

Everybody knows that white socks are a magnet for dirt, stains, and signs of wear and tear. They'll pick it up from inside your shoes, from your floors, and lord knows where else. Over time, those spots collect and take what was once shiny and new and make it stale and nasty. If your regular washing cycle isn't keeping them fresh, you have to up the ante a little bit.

First, pre-soak the offending pairs in one gallon of cool water and ¼ cup of bleach. Then, transfer them immediately to a washing machine and put them through with your regular detergent, hot water, and ¾ cup of bleach. After that, you can put them in the dryer (gentle cycle is best). Don't throw your colored clothing in here. This is for brights only.

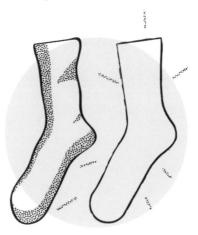

Note: If you're fresh out of bleach, you can substitute 1 cup of lemon juice for the pre-soak, and another cup plus 2 tablespoons of powdered dish detergent for the wash cycle.

KEEP YOUR COLOR

Socks are going to get washed. A lot. They pick up all kinds of mess from your feet and the world, and you want them staying fresh. But you also want them staying vibrant and colorful. Cleaning expert Jolie Kerr suggests avoiding any optical brighteners, as they'll actually cause your darks to fade faster. Speaking of darks, stick to a specific detergent like Woolite Darks to help maintain the color (a trick you can apply to the rest of your wardrobe). In general, to keep things looking as new as possible, separate your colors, roll with gentler detergents, and keep the wash cycle light to avoid too much agitation.

If you're dealing with a fine sock made of silk (like a Comme Si or a fancy Wolford one), be very delicate in washing. Oftentimes finer materials will last much longer if you go with handwashing and lay them flat on a towel to dry.

"I hang-dry my socks. It's a bit ridiculous, but I feel like it saves the elastic. It's the same reason I hang-dry my T-shirts—I don't want them to shrink."
—Jian DeLeon, editorial director, *Highsnobiety*

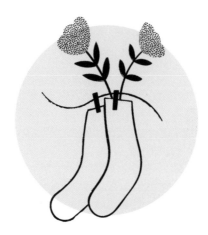

FRESH LIKE FLOWERS

Your feet are odor factories. It's okay; mine are, too. Same goes for whoever bought you this book. All that sweat, all that grime, and all those skin cells get transferred right to your socks. And before you know it, they're stinking up the whole joint. That's just life, but nobody said it had to be an eternity. There are a few things you can do to help here.

First, you can swap your regular detergent for an athletic/sports kind that's a little more engineered to fight odor. (HEX, Tide Sport, and Zero Odor work wonders!)

Second, you can toss in ½ cup of white vinegar during the rinse cycle. But if you need weapons-grade deodorizing, soak them in a bath of warm water with 2 cups of white vinegar (it's a miracle worker, I swear) and then wash as usual. If they still smell, buy some new socks. Their time may have finally come. I'm sorry for your loss.

FOLD FOR LIFE

The simple and most widely practiced way to store your socks, in what I'm sure is an impeccably neat drawer, is to ball them up together. The elastic helps to keep them in check, and this way you're not in danger of losing a single sock, rendering the other useless. But over time, this will wear out your socks and is not the most effective way of keeping them.

To save the elastic, some people even tie them together. This is a good thought, but ultimately it just strains wherever the knot is, doing more harm than good.

The best way is the KonMari way, popularized by organization titan Marie Kondo. For this method, lay matching socks on top of each other flat. If they're long socks (such as knee-highs), fold them in half once, twice, and then a third

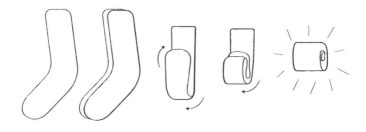

time if necessary to stand them up on their "sweet spot" (this will look like a little tent, with the middle of the sock tube facing up and out). For a regular, crew-length sock, fold into thirds before standing them up. And finally, for your shortest pairs, fold them tightly in half and place them upright in the drawer. They'll stick together well enough, save you space, and be free of any undue stress on the material.

THE SOCK DRAWER OF YOUR DREAMS

Once you've folded everything, you'll want to give it a proper home. For most of us, this is an underwear drawer that looks more like chaos than anything else. But life can be so much simpler! Place your upright folded pairs in the drawer so you can see them all at once. This will ensure that you're

not missing out on any especially great pairs that fall to the bottom of a drawer and that you'll spend less time searching for them in the morning. Imagine a bookshelf that's been laid on the floor; that's what you're going for.

"My sock drawer leads two different lives. Ankle socks: stored inside each other, creating what is effectively a loose cotton ball that maintains its pair status, clinging to each other for dear life. Long socks: folded per the KonMari method and stored facing up in a shoe box."
—Maura Brannigan, writer and editor

DARN REPAIRS

Generally speaking, I wouldn't recommend repairing socks. If you've got a hole in your favorite pair, my heart goes out to you, but my best advice would be to move on with some new ones. However, if for some reason, by some stretch of the imagination, you have a pair of socks that you absolutely cannot part with, you can try your hand at sewing them up, or darning them.

For this, you'll need a darning egg (a tennis ball will do if you don't have one), your busted sock, a thick thread that matches the material, and a darning needle.

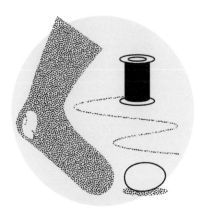

1. Push the ball to where the hole in your sock is. This will stretch the material a bit and create a more manageable working area.

2. Thread your needle and tie a knot at the end of it. You can make the thread whatever color you like, but generally, it's safe to match it to the sock itself.

3. Insert your needle into the sock at a spot close to the hole you're repairing. Pull it through, leaving the knot on the thread on the inside of the sock.

4. Find a spot at the edge of the sock hole on one side and thread the needle through once —the thread should still be on the outside of the sock. Leave the stitch slightly loose, not tight. Cross to the other side of the hole and repeat, keeping the stitch fairly slack.

5. Continue stitching from side to side, keeping them as close to the edges of the hole as possible. (This will help maintain the shape of the sock when you're finished.) When you've completed the criss-cross pattern, gently pull the end of the thread to close the hole.

6. Thread the needle through the sock one more time and pull it almost all the way through, leaving a loop on the outside of the sock. Take your needle and thread it through the loop and pull tight to create a knot.

7. Last time! Put the needle back through the sock, going in right near the knot you made and coming out about halfway through the stitches that closed the sock up (this will be on the front of the sock).

8. Pull tight and snip the excess.

LETTING GO

There comes a time in every sock's life when it simply can't go on anymore. If you invest in a quality pair and take care of them, this could be years! But even the most diligent of sock carers will be no match for time—fibers wear down, colors fade, and all that jazz. If you feel as though they're losing their mojo, you may have to make the call to let them go.

Here are five easy signs to look out for:

1. **Holes and Threadbareness:** You could take the time to repair these if you want, but that's often more trouble than it's worth. A sock with a hole in it is asking to be put out of its misery.

2. **Odor:** Athletic socks are especially susceptible to odors due to activity, but it can happen to any pair. If a stench won't go away after proper washing, you gotta toss them.

3. **Uneven Cushioning:** If you can sense a notable thinness or worn-out feeling, you may still have a couple of wears left, but the days are numbered. It's just age, and it happens to the best of us.

4. **Elastic Fatigue:** There's nothing worse than a sock that doesn't stay up. Nobody wants to spend their time pulling their socks up out of their shoe.

5. **Fading:** If you loved your bright blue patterned socks when you got them, but they've faded to a weird gray, it's worth it to replace them. It's more noticeable than you might think.

There are plenty of other reasons to put a pair out to pasture, of course. Somebody might drop ketchup all over them, for all we know. Just remember to treat socks as you would the rest of your clothing and you'll be just fine. And please, do not throw them in the garbage. There are plenty of uses for them and plenty of places to take them for a more environmentally friendly disposal. (More on that later.)

And remember, nothing puts a spring in your step like a brand-new sock.

CHAPTER FOUR

The Footmen

Socks on their own are a great time. You can dance in them, you can lounge in them, and they're generally just like a lighter version of a slipper. But they're really at full force when paired with some footwear. A soled mate, if you will. At the end of the day, what socks and shoes you match are really up to you. Style is a personal decision, so take all of this with a grain of salt, and consider it a jumping-off point. Always remember that there are very few absolutes when you're getting dressed.

Boots

The main thing to remember with boots is that your sock must be the proper length. As long as you're covering your bare skin, you should be good to go. This means you could wear anything, but since you're probably looking for warmth, stick with a standard or heavyweight option. A dress sock might slip, slide, and feel a little shaky.

Pair them with tube socks, boot socks, anything long enough to avoid leg-on-boot contact.

Regular Sneakers

Ah, sneakers, the everyman's shoe, an essential building block of any wardrobe, and my personal favorite. These call for something simple. If you want to keep it very normcore, stick with a basic tube sock, or perhaps an ankle sock with a little bit of flair or color on it. Just make sure you're working with a pretty standard-weight material, though you can go lighter if the sneakers are made of canvas or are a little more unconstructed.

Pair them with tube socks, ankle socks, colored socks, no socks.

Fancy Sneakers

Perhaps you're dealing with sneakers that are a little more premium than your garden-variety tennis shoe. These might be Common Projects, or something made from a fancy imported leather, or anything that costs half your rent. I commend you on your choice. Any casual sock will do you just fine here, but you can undoubtedly class it up a bit, especially if you're wearing them somewhere fancy—paired with a tuxedo at a black-tie wedding, for example. But if you're going with something a little more on the high-fashion spectrum, there is plenty of room to try something like an animal or geometric print.

Pair them with tube socks, ankle socks, colored socks, no socks, statement socks.

Heels

You don't often see heels and socks together, but it's a match for the ages, popularized by Hollywood movies, cool girls of cosmopolitan fashion capitals, and the rise of Instagram (probably). And if Dorothy can click her way back to Kansas in ruby slippers and sky-blue ankle socks, so can you. They could be knee socks, even! You'll definitely want to go with a finer material here, something a little more delicate than traditional cotton—perhaps merino or a fine-gauge cashmere.

Pair them with any fine-knit sock that's ankle length or longer.

Casual Dress Shoes

Loafers, brogues, ballet flats, derbys, and all of those some-what casual dress shoes can be tricky when it comes to socks. If you wear anything too thick, you risk stretching the leather, so you don't want any material that's too bulky. Stripes, subtle prints and patterns, and all solids are welcome here. Even a high-contrast—white socks with black shoes— à la Audrey Hepburn in *Funny Face*, is good to go.

Pair them with standard socks, ankle socks of an appropriate weight, or no socks at all.

Fancy Dress Shoes

All right, now we have officially entered upscale territory. This is probably the most natural match you can find. Just remember that almost always, dress shoes = dress socks. You want to opt for something that complements not just your shoes, but the rest of your outfit. You'll always be safe sticking in the same color family, but if you want to stunt a little bit with a pattern, just make sure nothing is too contrasting or clashy. (Don't go with electric green for a black suit, for example.) Remember that socks are a supporting player here—people should be admiring your dress, your suit, or your tux, not what's between you and your shoes. Keep it subtle and understated and lightweight.

Pair them with dress socks of any kind, as long as they don't distract from the whole vibe.

Sandals

All right. I know what you're thinking. And yes, this can go awry very, *very* quickly. It's a styling move often reserved for high-fashion runways that anybody can try, but you either know it works or you don't. Like the way you know you're left-handed or right-handed, you just *know*. It's best done when you're wearing pants—something about bare legs meeting socks and sandals screams, "I've given up on literally all things." It's also wise to keep it all monochromatic—high contrast is not your friend in this scenario. I'd avoid doing it with flip-flops. Stick to a double strap or something akin to a Birkenstock. But if you try it and it feels at all weird, just stop. That's a sign.

Pair them with a whole lot of confidence, non-contrasting socks, pants.

Remember, though: there are no hard-and-fast rules when it comes to getting dressed. What one person finds stylish, another might not.

CHAPTER FIVE

Everything Else Socks Can Do

There comes a time when we must say goodbye to socks. But despite their being one of the most requested items at homeless shelters, rules about accepting used socks vary from organization to organization. That leaves some questions when it comes to how to dispose of them in a sustainability-minded way. And sometimes, it's best to give them a second life as something else—a retirement, not a goodbye. And other times, when your sock has lost its mate prematurely, there are better things to do than throw it away.

Sock Puppets: Should you have a flair for the dramatic, the theatrical, or maybe just for crafts, you've probably made a sock puppet before. While they may not be up to the caliber of, say, the Muppets, they are a good way to keep yourself (or your kids) entertained for a few hours.

Rags: A sock that's lost its mate or has a hole or two is a perfect backup for a household cleaning rag. Spray that Pledge on the table, spritz those counters, and then wipe it all away. It's more fun if you wear the sock like some kind of cleaning gauntlet, but it is not required by any means.

The Overnight Play: Got dry hands? Socks can fix that! Before heading to bed, clean and exfoliate your hands and lotion them up with hand moisturizer. Pull your socks over your hands before going to bed to keep the moisture in and you'll wake up with baby-soft hands every time. (Naturally, you'll want to make sure the socks are clean.)

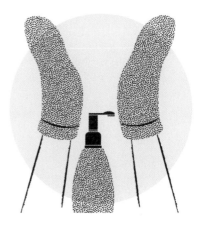

Leg Warmers: If you've got a pair of scissors and some socks you'd rather discard, or a pair that has a hole in the toes, you've got everything you need for leg warmers. I can't recommend this for daily wear, but if you've got an eighties party on the horizon, just cut them at the ankle and you're set.

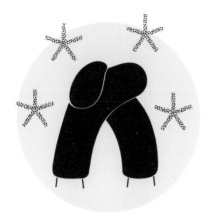

Gloves: When I was growing up, my father would run *very* early in the morning. When it was extra cold out, he'd wear socks as gloves to protect his hands, and it became a sort of a joke around town. I'm not sure if I'd be caught wearing old socks on my hands in public, but it's good to know it's an option.

Travel Bag: Not everybody is a world traveler with a perfect set of luggage and accessories, but almost everybody has a pair of socks. In a pinch, your valuables and tiny items can stay organized and safe in an errant sock.

The Sock Bun: Remember sock buns? Turns out your used (and cleaned) socks can make for the perfect hair accessory. Cut the toe off right at the seam to create an open tube on either side and put your hair in a ponytail. Then, roll the tube in on itself so it looks like a donut (or a bagel, if that's your thing) and move it to the base of your ponytail. Pull it up to the end of your hair and tuck the end of your hair through the bottom and you'll start to see things take shape. Now, roll the tube down to the base of your ponytail all while wrapping your hair around it to create a bun. Do some touch-ups, throw in a bobby pin, and you're in business.

Potpourri Bag: If you're looking to keep drawers, wardrobes, or any other nooks in your home or office a little fresher, your sock may be your savior. Fill it with potpourri or other things that smell heavenly, tie it shut with a ribbon, and pop it in the back, where it will be out of the way. It's like springtime in a drawer.

Ice Pack: If you're not into putting a cold compress of frozen peas right on your skin, socks can make the perfect barrier to keep things bearable. Alternatively, you can fill a sock with rice and zap it in the microwave for a hot pack.

Shoe Bag: Shoes can take quite a beating when you travel. They get knocked around all sorts of ways and can get scuffed quickly. A spare sock can serve as a shoe bag in a pinch to give them a little extra protection. Though I'd suggest investing in a standard dust bag if you travel often.

Beanbag: It's a DIY project, sure. But a lonely sock can make an excellent beanbag; you just need a little of that can-do spirit. All you need to do is cut the sock to your appropriate size, fill it up with rice, beans, or whatever you might think is a good filler, and stitch it up. If you're looking for a quick fix, you could also tie it off at the end. Cornhole, anyone?

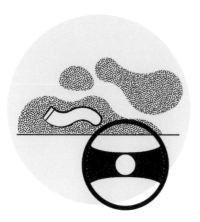

Car Window Hack: This is bizarre, but it works. Fill your sock to the ankle with silica kitty litter and place it anywhere in your car. By unholy magic, and I guess science, it will suck up moisture and help keep your windows from getting too fogged up. Miraculous socks!

The Perfect Dog Toy: Toss a tennis ball in there and you've got the perfect gift for man's best friend. Plus, you can swing it around in the air and let it fly, giving a whole new meaning to your usual games of fetch.

Cheap Bank: Who among us doesn't have a massive collection of spare change to put somewhere? No reason you can't put it in a sock. Save up for a while and you'll have a nice little nest egg in there.

The Dryer Ball Hack: If you didn't use all your tennis balls making a dog toy, drop one in a sock and throw it in the dryer with your next load of wash. It'll help keep things nice and soft.

Odd Storage: Socks are a good way to gather and organize all those little things that constantly go missing, such as game pieces, spare keys, or computer wires. At least you know when you eventually find them that they'll all be together.

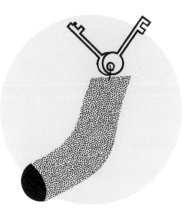

Cozy Coozie: I'm not sure who would be comfortable bringing an old sock so close to their face, but should you need a can coozie on the fly, you know what to do.

The Vacuum Trick: If you've got a lighter sock (or even a stocking), wrap it around the end of a vacuum hose to create a catchall filter. It might sound strange, but this will catch any small items you don't want disappearing into the bag—a helpful trick for finding a lost earring!

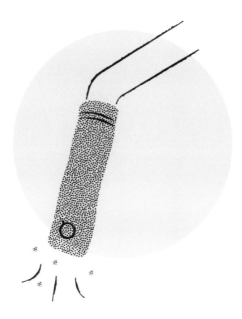

CHAPTER SIX

Famous Socks

SOCKROLL, PLEASE . . .

You may laugh at the idea of a sock being famous, but if you give it a second, I'm sure you'll think of at least one pair that's more well-known than the others. And yes, there's Socks the cat, a former first pet who captured hearts across the nation, but for this chapter, we're sticking with the ones that go on your feet. Tap your heels three times and away-we-go.

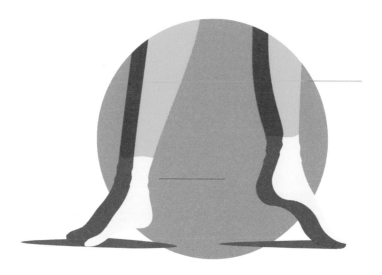

Slip and Slide: If we're ranking the fame of clothes from that scene in *Risky Business* with Tom Cruise's legendary slide, socks are probably at the bottom, behind the dress shirt, the underwear, and the glasses. But they get extra points because we all know sliding is only doable in socks. They did the work.

Not in Kansas Anymore: I'm willing to admit that the ruby slippers are probably more famous than the socks Dorothy wears with them, but since we're not talking about shoes that defy the laws of space and time, we'll stick with her iconic ankle socks. The image of the ruby-red slippers, the light-blue socks, and the Yellow Brick Road remains one of the most memorable in Hollywood.

Beware of Falling Houses: Dorothy may have ended up in the magic shoes, but that's only because somebody dropped a house on their previous owner. You never really get to know the Wicked Witch of the East, but you do see her famous striped stockings as they curl up under the house.

Mr. Pitt's Tubes: When *Seinfeld*'s Elaine Benes, one of history's greatest television characters, gets a job as Mr. Pitt's assistant, she has to run errands for him on the regular—the most memorable one being when she was sent all over town to find him the right socks. She and Mr. Pitt argue as she fails to find *just* the right pair, leading her to pass on a trip to Atlantic City. The episode is called "The Chaperone" and should be required viewing for all sock and/or television fans.

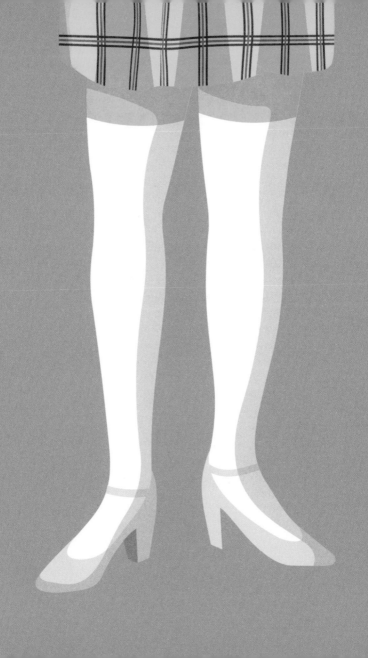

Cameo at the Val Party: No movie really defined the nineties quite like *Clueless* did. For anybody who came of age during that time, it's a must-see. The main character, Cher Horowitz, was a perfect avatar for the excess of the decade, best displayed by her sense of style. And if you look, you'll see that she's rarely seen without a pair of her trademark knee socks.

Lambchop the Puppet: You likely haven't thought about Lambchop, the young lamb puppet that kept kids entertained on PBS all through the nineties. She was perhaps the most famous sock puppet of all time, and certainly one of the wealthiest.

Color Counts: The classic comedy film *The Birdcage* has plenty of memorable scenes. But there's only one involving socks. Albert, played by Nathan Lane, drag queen, and partner to Robin Williams's Armand, attempts to mask his sexuality before meeting his son's girlfriend's conservative and homophobic parents. He trades his usual clothing for a simple suit. Armand and their son, Val, take a look at him as he crosses his legs to reveal a hot pink sock—"one does want a hint of color," he says. And he's not necessarily wrong.

Socks in a Pineapple Under the Sea: You don't have to watch *SpongeBob SquarePants* to know who he is. After all, he's the reigning king of memes and his own Broadway show these days. He's the only one in the world who can make wearing socks in the ocean look good.

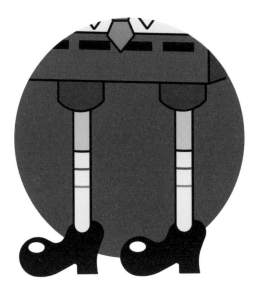

Socks and the City: When Man Repeller founder Leandra Medine Cohen was asked about some particularly iconic or famous socks, her answer was loud and clear: Carrie Bradshaw. As most of style-minded civilization knows, *Sex and the City*'s main character was never one to shy away from bold dressing, and that includes all kinds of socks—particularly over-the-knee ones.

A Scant Sock: We've covered some alternate uses for socks already, and yes, all of them are worth a try. But if you're looking for a somewhat more scandalous way to wear a sock, you might consider the Red Hot Chili Peppers and their famous "cock socks." Please attempt this only in the privacy of your own home or with consenting adults.

Funny Face, Funny Socks: Audrey Hepburn's memorable role of Jo Stockton in *Funny Face* opposite Fred Astaire has one of the best dance scenes in movie history. As she twirls around a Paris nightclub with two Frenchmen, you catch a glimpse of what would become a classic way to dress—black top, black cigarette pants, black loafers, and bright white socks.

Go Forth
and Sock On

Now that you're a sock expert, it's time to take all your new knowledge out for a test spin. But before you go out into the world and pick up an entire new sock wardrobe, remember a few things.

Your socks are going to be a representation of your style, and your style is completely your own. There's a lot of information in this book about how to wear, what to wear, and why to wear it, but ultimately everything is up to you. I myself prefer Bombas but am generally more sockless than not. If you want to wear a wild statement sock, go for it. Julee Wilson, a global beauty director, loves a statement sock: "I love a patterned sock. The flashier the better." Designer Rachel Antonoff has a similar philosophy when it comes to showing a little color: "A flash of bright red from under a chino is always a delight."

At the end of the day, you'll find what works for you. Jian DeLeon, the editorial director of Highsnobiety, swears by Nike Dri-FIT socks, having dabbled a bit in the world of bright and colorful socks for too long. Jenni Lee, who founded Comme Si, says to "treat socks like an accessory. Wear your socks to be seen; they have the ability to make any outfit more interesting."

That might work just as well for you, or you might find you're better suited to something else. But the most important thing is feeling comfortable in your own skin (and socks).

Resources

BRANDS YOU SHOULD KNOW

As we covered earlier, there are plenty of brands that make and manufacture socks, whether it's all they do or a part of a larger offering. You probably know your favorite sock brands by now, but in case you need some places to begin, here's a starter guide. (And it's by no means exhaustive.)

Ace & Everett: Quality socks that aren't boring, socks that aren't too loud. Aka great socks.

Adidas: Obviously they're a huge company with a focus on athletics and sports, and obviously they make great socks.

Anonymous Ism: Bright, patterned, insanely cool, and straight from Japan.

Bombas: One of the big of-the-moment sock brands that's focused on comfort, technology, and support. For every pair sold, they donate a pair to a shelter, nonprofit, or organization dedicated to helping the homeless, or in-need and at-risk communities.

Bonobos: A menswear brand founded on a better fit that makes socks with comfort, tech, and style in mind.

Brooks Brothers: If you want to class things up for your feet, swing by your neighborhood Brooks Brothers.

Comme Si: 100 percent Italian silk socks that are perfect for everyday wear and to bring a touch of style to any ankle.

The Elder Statesman: They make the world's best cashmere (it's also probably the most expensive, but you get what you pay for) and the world's most comfortable cashmere socks.

Falke: German engineering comes to socks, and they've been doing it since 1895.

Gold Toe: Simple, easy, and affordable.

Happy Socks: Printed! Patterned! All kinds of socks!

J.Crew: Found all over America, J.Crew is an easy spot to grab dress socks, casual socks, and anything in between.

L.L.Bean: Fine purveyor of American goods, a great spot for camp socks, boot socks, and outdoor socks.

Maria La Rosa: Finely crafted, very fancy, and worth the investment.

Merz b. Schwanen: Superior quality and craftsmanship, with a nod to old-world style. Never a bad call to grab some Merz.

Mr Porter: Not only a great place to shop for designer options of all kinds, but their private-label socks are second to none.

Muji: Muji has a huge offering of everything, socks included— try the marled ones.

Net-a-Porter: A website that offers the very finest of every- thing—not a bad place to sock shop.

Nice Laundry: Nice socks, too. A clever name!

Nike: They've got lots to offer, but there's an insanely loyal tribe to their Dri-FIT socks.

Noah: Some of the best three-stripe crew socks on the planet.

Pantherella: Socks straight from the UK. And any kind you could possibly imagine.

Paul Smith: Looking for some classic British humor and charm? Talk to Paul.

Ralph Lauren: A standard American go-to with a wide variety of options.

Turnbull & Asser: Fine tailoring, even finer socks.

Uniqlo: Japanese efficiency, ingenuity, and a great price all in one place.

Wigwam: For your everyday needs, particularly for tube socks, Wigwam is a great option.

Wolford: Known for high-end and high-quality socks and hosiery for women.

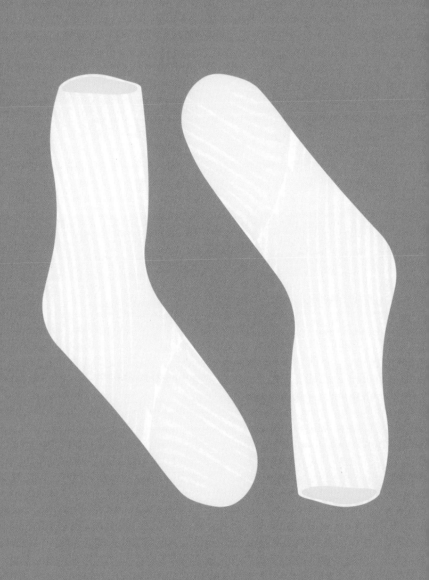

HOW TO DISCARD OLD SOCKS

If you've exhausted all possible uses for your old socks, some programs will allow you to upcycle or recycle them. Major retailers like Bombas, H&M, and the North Face have programs that will allow you to drop off used items of any kind, and some even offer discounts as an incentive. We should all remember that socks are the most requested items at homeless shelters across the country. If you plan to donate, it's best to check with your local locations and resources before deciding, as many operate in different ways.

A great way to get started is to visit the Bombas website's "Giving Back" section and looking at their 1,700+ giving partners across the United States. All you have to do is plug in your zip code and the range you're willing to travel, and they'll connect you with the proper location and even give you an email contact. Again, it's worth it to get in touch ahead of time to make sure you're clear on the rules for donating.

Acknowledgments

Thank you to Alex for always.

Thanks to my parents
for giving me feet with which
I could wear socks.

And to PJ for driving me to the mall.

And thanks to Liam and Amelia.

Editors: Sarah Massey and Samantha Weiner
Designer: Devin Grosz
Production Manager: Sarah Masterson Hally

Library of Congress Control Number: 2019939748

ISBN: 978-1-4197-4293-4
eISBN: 978-1-68335-810-7

Printed and bound in China
10 9 8 7 6 5 4 3 2 1

Abrams Image books are available at special discounts when
purchased in quantity for premiums and promotions as well as
fundraising or educational use. Special editions can also be created
to specification. For details, contact specialsales@abramsbooks.com
or the address below.

ABRAMS The Art of Books
195 Broadway, New York, NY 10007
abramsbooks.com

Ridin' the Ferry: The styling of Tess McGill in the early scenes in *Working Girl* was an ode to eighties style and commuting women all over the planet. Her over-the-tights tube socks and sneakers for her trip to the office were the perfect representation of being comfy while trying to stay professional. (Of course, she throws them off and puts on more business-friendly shoes at her desk.)

Newman's Own: Many men have made the white socks and classic loafers thing look good, but when it comes to style, it's nearly impossible to touch Paul Newman. It takes a certain confidence to carry it off, but if you've got the loafers and you've got a nice pair of white socks, you might as well go for it.
